Retirement

30 Days of Challenges & Activities That Will Guide You to a New Life!

Free membership into the Mastermind Self Development Group!

For a limited time, you can join the Mastermind Self Development Group for free! You will receive videos and articles from top authorities in self development as well as a special group only offers on new books and training programs. There will also be a monthly member only draw that gives you a chance to win any book from your Kindle wish list!

If you sign up through this link http://www.mastermindselfdevelopment.com/specialreport you will also get a special free report on the Wheel of Life. This report will give you a visual look at your current life and then take you through a series of exercises that will help you plan what your perfect life looks like. The workbook does not end there; we then take you through a process to help you plan how to achieve that perfect life. The process is very powerful and has the potential to change your life forever. Join the group now and start to change your life!
http://www.mastermindselfdevelopment.com/specialreport

Table of Contents

Introduction

Chapter 1: Welcome to Retirement!

Chapter 2: The Challenges of Retirement

Chapter 3: Getting in the Right Mindset for Retirement

Chapter 4: Activities for Retired Couples

Chapter 5: Dabbling Beyond the Bucket List

Chapter 6: Cheap Places to Live During Retirement

Chapter 7: 30 Fun-Filled Days of Retirement Challenges and Activities

Conclusion

© Copyright 2017 by _____ - All rights reserved.

The following eBook is reproduced below with the goal of providing information that is as accurate and as reliable as possible. Regardless, purchasing this eBook can be seen as consent to the fact that both the publisher and the author of this book are in no way experts on the topics discussed within, and that any recommendations or suggestions made herein are for entertainment purposes only. Professionals should be consulted as needed before undertaking any of the action endorsed herein.

This declaration is deemed fair and valid by both the American Bar Association and the Committee of Publishers Association and is legally binding throughout the United States.

Furthermore, the transmission, duplication or reproduction of any of the following work, including precise information, will be considered an illegal act, irrespective whether it is done electronically or in print. The legality extends to creating a secondary or tertiary copy of the work or a recorded copy and is only allowed with express written consent of the Publisher. All additional rights are reserved.

The information in the following pages is broadly considered to be a truthful and accurate account of facts, and as such any inattention, use or misuse of the information in question by the reader will render any resulting actions solely under their purview. There are no scenarios in which the publisher or the original author of this work can be in any fashion deemed liable for any hardship or damages that may befall them after undertaking information described herein.

Additionally, the information found on the following pages is intended for informational purposes only and should thus be considered, universal. As befitting its nature, the information presented is without assurance regarding its continued validity or interim quality. Trademarks that mentioned are done without written consent and can in no way be considered an endorsement from the trademark holder.

Introduction

Congratulations on purchasing your own copy of *Retirement*. Thank you so much for doing so!

If you purchased and are reading this book, I first would like to welcome you to your years of retirement! Within this book you will find a new light to what you think is a darkened time.

The following chapters will discuss one of the hardest chapters to transition to in life and how the remaining years after a life of hard work should not be dull and dreary, but rather should be fun, exciting and full of new adventures!

You will discover how important it is to live the remaining time you have here in this life to the fullest with plenty of fun and thrilling new activities.

The final chapter will explore a 30 day plan that is full of great ideas of activities, hobbies and new explorations you can take to discover yourself in a whole new way than you ever imagined at this age! If you are stuck in a rut of what to do during your years as a retiree, the contents of this book are waiting for your eyes to soak them in and start diving into the chapters loaded with activities that you now have plenty of time to do!

There are plenty of books retirement and what individuals can fill their lives with while they live their retired years on the market. Thanks again for choosing this one! Every effort was made to ensure it is full of as much useful information as possible. Please enjoy!

Welcome to Retirement!

Welcome to the last but not least stage of your life! Viewed negatively by many, retirement is a time for anxious excitement as you begin to wake up without that annoying alarm and can go about your day not having to worry about even getting dressed or heading to work. (Slightly kidding). Retirement is an entirely new thing to many and if you are anything like me, you have not put very much thought into what you are going to do with all that time that is being given to you or how you want to approach an entirely different picture regarding your finances. But there is no need to fear! While scary, retirement should be viewed as a time to enjoy yourself and dabbling in things that you did not previously have time for when you were young busy bee building your career and families.

Retirement is about doing leisure the right way and expanding yourself beyond the terms of your bucket list. Did you know that there are actually literal stages to leisure? That's right! It has been studied amongst those who are in the same boat as you!

4 Stages of Retirement Leisure

- **Stage 1 – Winding Down and Gearing Up**: The last 5 years of your working life is labeled as stage 1. This is the stage where most people are ready to retire. They are looking forward to not working and having time to relax and do the activities they wish they had time for during their working years.

- **Stage 2 – Liberation and Self-Discovery:** Those who have been in retirement for 2 years or less are enjoying their freedom and ample time. They have mostly adjusted to a work-less life and have started to recognize their identities outside of the workplace, becoming defined by other interests and hobbies.

- **Stage 3 – Greater Freedom and New Choices:** Retirees who are now 3-15 years into retirement have fully embraced their new identities and feel content and happy in their final stage of life. Anxiety of retirement has left and been replaced with confidence and happiness.

- **Stage 4 – Contentment and Accommodation:** Retirees 15 or more years in retirement are striving towards optimum health and continuing their path towards everlasting independence. They enjoy time with family rather than spending a bunch of time creating new hobbies and dabbling in new experiences.

The Challenges of Retirement

Financial Challenges

Retirement for many people is as scary as it is exciting. You have worked your entire life to earn enough to live your remaining years peacefully and without worry. But now a days, there are more challenges arising in regards to the community of retirees. Throughout your working life you have accumulated assets to aid you in cushioning your retirement. From participating in the 401(k) plan and maybe even establishing yourself in an IRA or other retirement plan, despite how much you have contributed, times are continuously changing, which is why it is absolutely crucial to plan out how to convert your assets into the right kind of income.

Many retirees find themselves only having Social Security and their retirement savings to get them by for the remaining years of life. Unlike previous generations, you may not be under a pension plan from where you worked, so you might be totally on your own when it comes to overcoming these challenges when stepping into retirement.

Longevity

We all have a chance to live longer or shorted than anticipated. A recent study conducted in 2015 by the Society of Actuaries showed that a 55 year old male has around 76% chance to live until the age of 90, while a female of the same age has 82% chance of living to their 90's. What does this mean? It means that you may spend just as much time in retirement as you did working in your career. Creating enough income to cover day to day expenses for 30 or more years is a daunting thought and task, especially in a world where there are fewer opportunities available to those of retirement ages to earn income.

Volatility

Environmental disasters and other events are not predictable, such as earthquakes, tsunamis, 9/11. When these types of events occur, you can almost always predict an impact on the financial markets. These events are always a possibility, but should not hinder your ability to trade your assets. However, you should be wary. Trading now a days is completed 100% electronically and at the speed of light. In order to get the most bang for your buck, ensure that the climate of conductive trading is at least somewhat balanced to produce a greater volatility.

Inflation

Inevitably, the prices of goods and services increase annually each year. Even though the inflation rate has dropped and maintained in recent years, hovering around 1-3%, it can still have an impact on your purchasing power. For example, today's $1,000 may only be able to purchase $550 in goods 30 years from today with a 2% increase in inflation. With 3%, that grand $1k will only be able to buy you $400 worth of goods and/or services. And who is to say inflation won't exceed past 2-3%? That means the results could greatly impact your ability to live without stress. Retirees living on a fixed income can run into many difficulties when it comes to making ends meet later down the road. And the goods and services that tend to go up the most are those utilized by retirees themselves.

Taxation

If you were within the high tax bracket for the majority of your life, retirees must be aware of where their assets are invested. Hedge funds and mutual fund managers tend to not consider taxes when seeking out profits. The turnover of portfolios can be high and short-term capital gains, which are taxed at regular income rates and tend to be generated in abundance. Mutual funds also have the potential to create "phantom income", which means its distributions or capital gains are reinvested in additional fund shares. You never see them, but are still continuously taxed on them. There are many investors that find themselves paying taxes of distributions of capital gains when their other fund shares have majorly decreased in value within the year.

Leaving Legacies to Your Loved Ones

While there are retirees already stressing out about how they are going to live in their elderly years, there are plenty who have no concerns when it comes to making ends meet during their retirement. However, every single retiree has the challenge of leaving a legacy to loved ones. In fact, this is typically a primary concern, especially if it is related to estate taxes. As much as 40% reduction to the estate tax can occur, depending on where you live. Erosion is a profound issue.

How to Combat These Financial Challenges

Back many years ago, the go-to strategy as you reached retirement was to reallocate your portfolio(s) from equities to fixed income and live off of the interest it generated. Today, the all time low of interest rates and increase of life expectancies have eradicated this method.

One strategy to consider as you reach retirement age is the 4% solution. You can avoid the total depletion of your little nest egg by withdrawing 4% per year from your assets. This strategy is not foolproof by any means because it is based around the possibility of living only an additional 25 years after initial retirement. There is a great possibility you could live longer and run out of money to live off of.

Another strategy is to identify your sources of income that is guaranteed to you. Look into variable annuities that are issued by insurance companies that offer professionally managed investment options that are moldable to shape around your life. Similar to the IRA or 401(k) plans, variable annuities have assets that grow tax-deferred until they go to be withdrawn by the owner of the contract. This means when it comes time for you retire, you can choose to receive life contingent income distributions. Depending on the options you choose, you have a good chance of being able to receive income that is guaranteed to last as long as you live.

What to Do with ALL This Time?

This question is often referred to as "the retirement problem." There is a combination of excitement paired with anxiety within those that are approaching retirement age. It is exciting to have free time and not be bound by work and its deadlines, yet, anxiety takes hold when it comes time to bear the questions of what to do with all the ample time you are about to have and how to figure out how much you can and can't spend. Much of the population imagines what their retirement will be early on and create big plans of what they wish to do with all that time that is still within their budget. Once we reach retirement age however, people tend to have major doubts of what is to come next for them and their lives. Another realization for retirees is recognizing that this is the last stage of their lives. Throughout their youth, they knew deep down that life is short and flies by fast, but during those years they were busy building careers and families, which kept the emotional recognition of this inevitable fact at bay. This is enough to make anyone scared of the future and the anxiety of trying to make the best of what they have left come to light.

While time and money go hand in hand, money is the more practical of the two concerns. Many retirees become more anxious about having enough money to get by rather than how they will be spending the remainder of their time here on earth. More and more retirees are becoming less sure about what their income during retirement is going to be and where it is going to take them. Money is not all one needs to have a successful retirement. In saying this, it is important for those approaching retirement to have more than just a financial plan. They must also have some idea of what they plan to do with the rest of their time in order to be engaged in the last stage of their life while still being productive.

That being said, it is important to get to know yourself. For many, leaving the workplace you have known your entire life can be frightening. Retirement is kind of like stepping into your freshman year of high school all over again. It is stepping out of your comfort zone and into a new era. You may feel that you are stripped of your self and what you thought you were, especially if you kept the mindset that you were only who you were in your career. Their may be a period of grief from the job itself as well as a disconnection of friendships and relationships you built over your working years. It is important to get busy in terms of getting to know yourself in order to know what you wish to do when your years in your career are over so that you can continue to live life successfully and prosperously.

Take the time to self-reflect on your life and yourself as a whole. What do you enjoy about your job the most? What do you like to do the most during your hours away from work? If you have no idea, perform this mental exercise. Imagine that your office is closed for an entire week. Ask yourself what you would do with that time off? If you have no clue, think about your hobbies or activities you wish to take up and experiment with. Think about places to volunteer. Things like this. What makes your soul light up? What makes you tick? It is important to dig deep in reference to this, because you are going to have a lot of time to kick back and relax, but I assure you that just relaxing will not suit you in the long run. Are there things you have always wanted to learn? Are there ways you wish to make the world around you a better place?

Inevitably, there are going to be things you pursue in your retirement age that you are not good at or you do not like as much as you thought you would. It is important to seek out classes to better specific skills so that you are not constantly put down by not being able to accomplish what you wish to.

If you are someone that has the urge to continue working, then perhaps you should consider a phased retirement, which means you can work part-time to still earn a paycheck and keep yourself semi-busy as you still draw from your retirement benefits. This will keep you engaged in your social life and contribute to perhaps a longer life, for work of many kinds keeps your wits about you!

But for many individuals, they have had their sights on retirement for a long time and know exactly how they wish to live out the remainder of their life. Most of these people contribute to causes they are passionate about that they have not had the time for throughout their younger years, whether it is helping with disaster relief, autism, food insecurity, etc. Or they venture into things that utilize the skills they have been performing for years to help others. Those with a "second career" tend to enjoy their retirement more than those that hated what they did for a living and see retirement as a time to do nothing end enjoy themselves. Those engaged in these types of second careers are more energized and feel much more fulfilled as they used the knowledge they acquired throughout their life to bring new meaning to the lives of others and beyond.

So, if you are approaching retirement or have just stepped into it, what are activities, hobbies, second careers, etc that you wish to conduct the remaining years of your life in? The remaining chapters in this book are all about branching out and trying new things, putting the skills you already have to the test and experiencing life with ample time under your belt in the most fulfilling way possible. Now that the depressing chapter is over, good luck! I hope you come across ideas that stand out and that you feel great trying them out!

Getting in the Right Mindset for Retirement

Retirement is much more fun than you have heard from your coworkers, family, friends, doctors, etc. The sky is truly the limit! When it comes to you picturing a successful retirement, I'm sure you envision financial stability, traveling the world and relaxing in various ways. While money, travel and leisure are key components to retirement, there is one aspect that many approaching retirees have yet to think about.

Having the right kind of mindset to successfully enjoy your time in retirement is a crucial part of retirement planning. While it is important to plan out your retiring years financially, it is just as crucial to psychologically prepare yourself for this stage of life as well. In order to get yourself in the proper mindset, one must realize what it truly means to take this step financially, psychologically and emotionally. In fact, establishing the right mindset is just as important as ensuring your financial stability.

Things to consider as you approach retirement:

- Why are you retiring in the first place, besides age of course? Many times, people think they should retire just because of the simple fact they have reached age 65. There are many other more valid reasons to retire, but you should be consciously aware of the particular reason you are deciding on retirement.

    - Has your job become too physically demanding?
    - Is your job too stressful? If so, are there ways to remove or combat those stresses without having to retire?

- What are you planning to do with the loads of time you are about to receive? Having ample time to do as you wish seems fantastic, but think about the fact that retirement may last just as long as you're working years. This leaves a lot of time for just leisurely doing nothing with your life. Think seriously about how you wish to spend your remaining days before you become too old to enjoy the things that you wish you had done. Write down answers that suit you. Do not live off of someone else's feelings and thoughts for retirement.

- Does your career define who you are as a person? Throughout our working years, we fail to see how tied we are to our career when it comes to determining who we are as a human being. We are not just computer specialist, brokers, real estate agents, accountants, etc. Each of us are human beings that should not let our careers determine who we are for life. Sadly, letting go of a career can be difficult, more so than many realize. This is why many people who retire convert to a second mini career that leaves them to work part time. This includes work such as volunteering, teaching, mentoring or consulting, just to name a few. They have decided to take the knowledge they have acquired throughout their life and put it to good use, helping others and bettering the world around them.

- If you can, it is of good practice to try mini-retirements before you actually take the initiative to retire. Use vacation time as a trial run for retirement. If your retirement vision is all about relocation, spend your time during retirement trial runs in new locations.

- It is recommended to be flexible during retirement, especially in the early stages. Rent instead of buy and move around a bit to get a taste for newness. Don't go out and buy condos, RV's or other big purchases unless you know for sure that it will suit you during your time in retirement.

- Remember that if you have a spouse, retirement should be something done as a team. This doesn't mean you necessarily have to retire at the same time, but you should talk about each of your visions for retirement and what you both want out of it. You should be ready to accommodate differences, for you will be together a lot more than when you both were at work. It should be seen as a time to enjoy one another thoroughly, for you will both have free time to spend as you wish. Just be prepared for the adjustment and to give one another space as needed. It is best to have a gap of at least 6 months when retiring, meaning one of your retire and the other waits at least this period of time before retiring. This will help make the transition easier for both of you, for one will have their sea legs equipped by the time the other retires.

Methods of Getting in the Right Mindset

Law of Attraction

The Law of Attraction is a law that states that whatever we think to be true, simply is. If we constantly think negative, we will attract negative things to our lives and vice versa. The Law of Attraction is all about magnetizing to us who we are and wish to be. It is about giving off the right vibrations that will then bring positive things to our lives. So, think positive, even if your bank balance may not be what you wish it to be. The more positively you use your wisdom and sense of faith in good ways, the more possibilities you will have for good things to come your way during the leisure time of your life!

Meditation

In order to really enjoy retirement, physical and mental health are as vital as ever. Continue to begin your days with a good attitude. Make time for walks, going to the gym, etc. Meditate for at least 30 minutes each morning in order to get the feel-good energies flowing within you.

Affirmations

As vital as it is to fuel the conscious mind, it is just as important to feed our subconscious minds as well. Repeating something positive and uplifting each morning when we wake and before hitting the hay at night can help us get on the right path in the direction we wish to go.

Surround Yourself with Uplifting, Like-Minded Individuals

Just like throughout the entirety of your life, you probably found that you were a better version of yourself when you gave way to positive people and got rid of those that held you down. The same goes for in retirement as well. Steer clear of those that will suck away your positive energies and fuel your bad habits. Find people who think like you do, that support you and provide you with upbeat energies. No reason to spend the remaining time you have here on this planet surrounding yourself with negativity and harmfulness.

Pursue Your Passions

Think about all the things you loved that you may not had very much time to do growing up and during the years engulfed in your career. Retirement is a perfect time to pick up favorite hobbies and dabble in new passions. Go conquer your passions head-on with confidence! It is never too late to delve deep into the things that bring you joy.

Financial Boosters

Just like it is never a better time like the present to get involved in your passions, the same goes for extending yourself out into creative passive income ideas. If you have limited finances during retirement, seek online business opportunities that do not require you to invest a bunch of money. There are also numerous ways now thanks to the ever-changing internet to educate yourself when it comes to delving into various ways of creating income online from the comfort of your own home.

Continue to Stay Busy

While the leisure of being able to take a few moments of time to yourself without the demands of work or family is nice, you hopefully have much more time than just a couple of years of retirement. In order not to become frustrated and bored with life, you need to remain busy. Here are a few ideas to remain productive while still enjoying the time you have earned to enjoy your life.

- **Write your memoirs** – Whether your write in a journal or in the form of letters to loved ones, record any past adventures, experiences or memories you feel are worth being remembered for lifetimes. If writing letters, choose specific family members to write them to. Utilize the wisdom that you think will suit that individual the most as they make their way through life. You can also take up a memoir writing class!

- **Read books** – I am sure you have a list of at least a few books that you have wanted to read but have not had the time to do so during all those years in your career. Whether you have a list of potentials you wish to read or not, head down to your local library and surf through the shelves for books that catch your eye. Ensure that you read a variety of books. There are also plenty of books that are on audio to listen to as you relax or websites like Amazon or Indigo that can ship books you want to indulge in right to your doorstep! There are many avenues now a days to get to the books you wish to soak up!

- **Learn a new language** – Acquiring a new language is a great way to exercise your brain in order to keep your mental abilities clear and sharp. Rosetta Stone or Duolingo are great places to start and include many varieties of languages to choose from. If you prefer to learn in a class-room type setting, there are many language classes than you can pursue as well. Learning a new language helps you overall in your ability to communicate with a variety of different people.

- **Weekly physical activities** – Staying active is now important for retirees than ever in their life. There are many different activities to choose from to become involved in, such as golfing, swimming, jogging, etc. There are plenty of classes that seniors can participate in. Or you can take lessons when it comes to learning a new physical activity

- **Join a club** – There are lots of various clubs that tend to the interests of many. From bridge club, reading club, golf club, church club, etc, look around your community for different clubs that suit your fancy.

- **Learn a new skill by taking a class** – Hone in on hobbies that you want to improve and look for classes that can help you learn the skills necessary for you to successfully conquer those hobbies.

There are many different ways to spend your time in retirement, remain busy and enjoy yourself all at once! The remaining chapters of this book will bring to light many more activities and hobbies you can try out.

Activities for Retired Couples

If retirement wasn't already a fun and exciting time, imagine being able to spend more valuable time with the love of your life, doing things and experiencing new things together! Hobbies and activities can bring married couples closer together because it is way easier to communicate when side by side than face to face. Also, the more time spent together doing activities enjoyed by both parties, the more goodwill that is built up which makes is easier to conquer bigger issues within the marriage as age continues to take hold. Also, activities that are done together help in the building and creation of memories that will last a lifetime. You feel more like a team and begin to find the people that met and announced vows to one another when you were much younger. You find your youthful selves again at the ripening age of retirement and you feel closer than ever before, even during your working careers. And the best part? The things that bugged you about one another seem to vanish!

Plus, it is much more fun to experience things and start new hobbies with another person! It is fun to spend time with your spouse outside of your house and comfort zone. And it is more exciting to learn new things together as well. The best part about experiencing new activities and hobbies is that both of you do not have to enjoy it to the same extent. The goal is to spend time together rather than seriously dabble in the hobby itself.

It is important to take the time for you both to make lists of things you wish to do or want to try. The list within this chapter is a great place to start! Pick three things that catch your eye off this list or off your own personal list. Exchange lists and choose one thing you would like to do or try from your spouse's list. Now all you have to do is figure out which one you wish to begin first!

Classes to Take Together

- Theology
- Natural Herbs/Health
- Financial Planning
- Investing
- Computer Software
- Cooking

Places to Volunteer Together

- Refugee welcome center
- Food bank or other outreach center
- Hospital conducting visitations
- Nursing home

- Youth organizations – Boy/Girl Scouts, Big Brothers/Big Sisters, 4-H, local school, etc.
- Local art organizations – theatre, local dance groups, local symphonies, museum, art gallery
- Church – worship, building upkeep, finances, etc.

Things to Collect as a Couple

- Memorabilia from certain periods of time/cultural trends/historical events
- Old magazines, comic books, books
- Sea glass, seashells, driftwood
- Stamps or coins
- Local art
- Art by a particular artist

Hobbies that Product Income

- Catering
- Photography/Videography
- Start a blog about a topic you both like and can contribute to
- Start up an etsy/ebay business
- Yard sale/flea marketing
- Finding and refurbishing items
- Building/painting furniture

Domestic Hobbies for Couples

- Home improvement
- Painting
- Homesteading
- Cooking
- Gardening

Educational Hobbies for Couples

- Touring wineries
- Planning an educational trip
- Tracing back one another's family trees
- Learning about local history
- Become tour guides
- Tourist art galleries or nearby local historical sites

Games for Couples

- Strategical video games

- Bridge club
- Euchre club
- Board games
- Puzzles
- Chess league

Events to Attend Together

- Film festivals or film clubs
- Special museums or art gallery exhibits
- Music performances
- Plays, dance performances, comedians
- Sporting events
- NASCAR races
- Go on a date – Being able to leave work behind also leaves behind the excuses of not being able to go out with your hubby. It is important to remember that dates and surprises within relationships and marriages are still vital at any age!

Sporty Indoor Activities for Couples

- Zumba classes
- Square Dancing/Line Dancing
- Irish Dancing
- Ballroom Dancing
- Rock Climbing (indoor)
- Bowling
- Swimming
- Racquetball/Squash
- Aquafit class
- Yoga class
- Working out/weightlifting

Outdoorsy Activities for Couples

- Foraging
- Metal detecting
- Photography
- Rock climbing
- Target Practice
- Skiing
- Join a co-ed sports league
- Jogging/Training for Marathon
- Biking

- Tennis
- Golfing
- Windsurfing
- Sailing
- Canoeing
- Snowmobiling
- Kayaking
- Hunting
- Fishing
- Bird Watching
- Hiking

You are halfway done!

Congratulations on making it to the halfway point of the journey. Many try and give up long before even getting to this point, so you are to be congratulated on this. You have shown that you are serious about getting better every day. I am also serious about improving my life, and helping others get better along the way. To do this I need your feedback. Click on the link below and take a moment to let me know how this book has helped you. If you feel there is something missing or something you would like to see differently, I would love to know about it. I want to ensure that as you and I improve, this book continues to improve as well. Thank you for taking the time to ensure that we are all getting the most from each other.

Dabbling Beyond the Bucket List

There are many different avenues when it comes to retirees figuring out how they wish to live there final stage of life. That being said, there are many fun ways to truly enjoy the ample time you are about to have given to you! While there may be no more work deadlines or demands, your own personal life should demand from you one thing: to live the remaining years of your life to the absolute fullest! Experiencing and learning new things! It is time to go beyond the extent of your bucket list and to dabble in new things that will help your inner you shine!

Outdoor Retirement Ideas

- **Metal detecting** – This activity can also be done with grandkids in toe! Metal detectors are cheap and start at $50 and up. You can take them to the beach, the park and other public areas and find numerous kinds of treasures that are right beneath your feet! They can be taken anywhere around the world and can be a great hobby, especially if you like to collect unique trinkets.

- **Go on a road trip** – If you have access to a car or RV that you are still capable of driving, it is time to get the map out and pick a few places to visit that you have yet to have time before now to travel to and explore. This will introduce you to new sights and brand new people, as well as being able to feast your eyes on amazing sights.

- **Travel to another country** – Whether you have a country in particular that you have wanted to see or a distant relative you have not had the time to travel and visit with in ages, retirement is a good time to travel abroad.

- **Outdoor craft shows and flea markets** – Vendors at these shows are eager to share their expertise and findings with you, which can lead you to acquire valuable knowledge and perhaps intrigued and interested in what they do. This is a great way to discover new hobbies that you otherwise may not have thought about. These shows are also amazing venues to gather and collect items at half the cost of other places. Events like craft shows give elders ideas to host their own, bringing their communities together as well.

- **Outdoor theater/concert** – Many communities have some sort of festivals, productions or musical events of some sort or another. Retirees can either watch or be participants in the events. If you are a senior attending these events, they are typically free!

- **Kite flying** – This is a great activity to partake in when watching the grandkids. But you can also join kite clubs and participate in kite flying with others your age as well. There are activities that involve building your very own kite to challenges such as kite flying races. Or you can simply enjoy the outdoors in your own free time by kite flying.

- **Garden party** – This is by no means just for elderly women! There are a number of organizations that host these events or you can even host them yourself. If you have a patio perfect for a garden or somewhere in your community that could use a little sprucing up and a pop of color, a garden party is a perfect activity to indulge yourself in!

- **Picnic** – This can be hosted anywhere with outdoor space. Picnics are very popular among the retired community and it is quite simple to do. Especially if it is done in a pot-luck manner where many people come and bring their own edible creations.

- **Yard games** – There are a variety of easy to play games that let retirees come outdoors and get a little physical exercise while having fun!

    - *Cup and ball* – Yes, they still make the old fashioned wooden cup and ball games, where the ball is attached to a cord. Have a friendly competition to see who can get their ball in the cup the most times.

    - *Pickle Ball* – This is becoming a very popular game among the elderly communities, and there are people even clear in their 90's that enjoy participating! It is kind of like tennis, but the ball involved bounces more like a ping long ball. This light ball is used along with a paddle racket.

    - *Horseshoes*

    - *Ring toss*

    - Croquet

    - Shuffleboard

    - Bad mitten

    - Walking Races

    - Water Balloon Toss

    - Yard Darts

    - Lawn/Patio Bowling

    - Beach Volleyball

- - Frisbee Target Toss
  - Ladder Toss

- **Boat Rides** – If you choose to live anywhere during retirement, somewhere near a body of water is a splendid idea! This not only makes for a beautiful scenery to feast your eyes on, but leads to other activities that can only be performed in the water, such as boating.

- **Fishing** – There are seniors of many sexes and ages that enjoy an afternoon of leisurely fishing. They love talking about their fishing extrusions and documenting what they have caught.

- **Botanical garden/conservatory** – Gardening is an all time favorite hobby that many of those that are retired take up. From building the foundation for a great garden to strolling through what they personally made, maintaining gardens is just one of those activities that are satisfying and easy to share with others.

- **Garden club** - Join one of these clubs in order to share your successful gardening skills with others who wish to broaden theirs!

- **Clay pot painting** – When it comes to having the best garden in town, many more individuals are seeking creative minds to come up with ideas to help sprout the perfect pop of color in their gardens. This can include painting plain ole clay pots into something wonderful! Whether you are painting them for your own garden/patio or to sell, painting is a good relaxing activity to take up.

- **Berry picking** – This gives way for retirees to get the exercise they need as they walk around and collect bright colored, delightful berries. Eat your gatherings with others or find a recipe that involves your delicious findings.

- **Visit an apple orchard** – There are many places that have orchards that the community can visit and pick their own fruit from, apple orchards being one of the most popular. It can be educational, fun and fruitful, for many of the people use the apples in baking and creating other things.

- **Visit a pumpkin patch** – These are typically the most abundant during the fall season and it is a fun extrusion to take the grandkids on as well. From picking out a pumpkin to learning how to paint/carve one, there are a variety of fall activities that can be done at the pumpkin patch. Hayrides, cider sipping and corn mazes are just a few more!

- **Hiking** – Hiking is an outdoor activity enjoyed by many, giving retirees ample exercise and time spent outdoors. It can be done at zoos, lakes, mountains, parks, etc.

- **Treasure/Scavenger Hunt** – These types of activities are really fun for the elderly and can be done alongside the youthful population as well.

- **Mini Golf/Putting** – Golf seems to be a sport that many retirees take up. Either they already know the sport well or like to learn how to play it at retirement age. There are also a number of contests to participate in once you hone your golfing and putting skills a bit.

- **Archery** – For retirees who still have much of their strength and mobility left in them, archery is a great outdoor activity to learn! This helps one hone their ability to aim and focus on a target. There are also archery clubs that you can find to join.

- **Bird watching** – While this hobby means taking a bit of time to study birds and their habits, its' among the more popular, especially among the elderly community. There are many places that actually have bird watching groups and there are departments that provide learning materials on different species of birds.

- **Photography** – Photography is one of those skills that you can quickly acquire and it doesn't mean that you have to have an expensive camera to take great shots. There are many people that teach photography for a living. Join a club and snap away!

- **Be a campground host** – This is a great idea, especially for retirees who decide to travel. In exchange for free camping, they can help park managers and other campers with their chores, lead nature walks, clean up campsites, collect fees and offer to welcome in new park guests. While some do this activity for fun, others do it to help stretch their dollar out a bit more!

- **Set up dates with your kids/grandkids** – Depending on how you like to spend your time, this can be either an indoor or outdoor activity. If you are a grandparent who has not been able to spend as much time with family thanks to working so much, retirement is the perfect opportunity to catch up on lost time.

    - Visit a zoo
    - Go to the movies
    - Take a walk
    - Play video games
    - Go to a museum

- o   Trying cooking or baking together
- o   Teach one another a skill

- **Rediscover your spirituality** – While reconnecting your soul to your spirit, this can be done either indoor or outdoors, but connecting with nature is a big plus. While we live through our middle ages between our 30's-50's, we tend to lose sight of the bigger picture thanks to being so busy with the hustle and bustle of everyday life and working. Retirement is a time to redefine your spirituality and to become engulfed in yourself and your soul.

- **Get moving!** – Independence and the capability of mobility go hand in hand. If you don't use it, you lose it and at a much faster rate when you are aging. There are certain physical aspects you took majorly for granted while you were younger that you are no longer capable of, but that doesn't mean you have to stop moving. Exercise is as close as you are going to get to a miracle drug. It assists you in managing blood sugars, blood pressure, pain and fatigue, only to name a few benefits. It can even help you boost your memory power. Remember that exercise should be fun! If you do not like certain exercises, stop doing them and find something you life to do.

  - o   Tai Chi
  - o   Swimming
  - o   Yoga
  - o   Walking
  - o   Cross-Country
  - o   Downhill Skiing
  - o   Rowing
  - o   Kayaking
  - o   Bicycling
  - o   Tennis

- **Adopt a pet** – If no other activities get you motivated, then it may be time to think about adopting a pet. Whether it is a dog, a cat, a bird or a gerbil, having someone other than another human to bond and spend time with that depends on you can be a great motivator when it seems that life is boring. Check in with your local animal shelter first to see the pets they have available for adoption. You are not only helping yourself out but you are helping a furry friend in need all at the same time!

- **Join an outdoor sports team** – If you love sports and still have the energy to muster up for some competition, there are plenty of avenues that can land you back on the playing field. Check into your community's recreation department to sign up for senior teams.

Indoor Retirement Ideas

- **Help in the classroom** – If you have always liked being around children and young adults, perhaps you can try your hand at teaching or helping a teacher. From tutoring to being a teacher's aid, there are many ways to get involved in your local school system.

- **Become a teacher** – It is becoming more prevalent to not need a teaching degree in order to become certified as a K-12 teacher. While requirements vary, it doesn't take too much time to become certified in order to teach in a subject you are passionate about.

- **Hone your cooking skills** – Even if you think you are a master chef, there is always some room for improvement. Join a cooking class or baking club and learn from the techniques of others to make way for brand new techniques to use right in your kitchen!

- **Join the Peace Corps** – While you may think you are too old to join such an organization, there is no age limit when it comes to joining this one! Your time of volunteer service can last anywhere from three months to two years and you have the chance to choose the country you wish to serve in, the type of work you will be doing and when you can depart.

- **Join a chorus** – It is time to put that amazing voice to the test other than while in the shower. If you are unsure where to begin your singing journey, there are typically many types of various singing groups in many areas, looking for new people to join their group. While some choirs take the people they let join their groups very seriously, there are some more lighthearted groups that sing just for fun. Find a group that suits you!

- **Dabble in the arts** – It's no lie when I was that creating art helps feed your soul and inner being. Many individuals who retire seek out various classes to take to learn or relearn skills, such as painting, drawing and crafting. There are bound to be academics and workshops you can get yourself involved in around the areas you live.

- **Write out your memoirs** – Are there things about your life that you wish for your kids, grandkids and great-grandkids and beyond to know about you? Retirement is the perfect time and place to recall good and bad memories and write them down. Whether it's in a journal or in letters to particular family members, it is a great way to pass the time while doing something constructive that the entire family will enjoy for generations to come.

- **Construct your family tree** – If no one has bothered with putting together your family tree or record the ancestry of your family, perhaps it is time to use some of your time in retirement to do just that! Dedicate time to conduct adequate research in your family's history, contacting immediate and distant family members so that you can create a comprehensive tree of family connections. There are also online tools that can help you in doing this. The goal here is to have something your entire family can enjoy for generations to come and something that is easy to add on to when you pass.

- **Learn cooking in a whole new way** – Whether you are a master chef or have never learned to cook or bake very well, retirees find that taking up a cooking class or participating in cooking/baking competitions is very rewarding. If you are already a pretty decent cook, hone your skills and acquire a new skill set, like learning how to cook French or Thai cuisine.

- **Explore your city's history** – It is natural for retirees to feel a deep connection with the past, including history. Retirement is a good time to get to know the history behind the city you reside in. Take up a history class of some kind that delves into the inner workings of your town's past and helps you to explore and have fun acquiring knowledge along the way.

- **Volunteer at the public library** – Your own public library or a school library loves the extra helping hands of the retired. Retirees have a great respect for the world of books and volunteering at your library can be a great way to give back to your community too. It's a good place to meet new people and develop new relationships as well!

- **Become a hospice volunteer** – There are plenty of long term care facilities that need more helping hands and big hearts. While helping those who are dying is not for everyone, those who are will be forever grateful to have someone visit them and help them each day as they close the final chapter of their lives.

- **Rediscover your love of reading** – Many people love to read but never find the time when their lives were so busy. Retirement is the perfect time to find that list of books you have wanted to read for so long and curl up with a good book as you relax. Now that you have more free time, visit the library, scrounge about at flea markets or book sales. And make sure you have a cozy chair or area to read in.

- **Volunteer at your local animal shelter** – Volunteering at non-profit places like animal shelters is a great way to spend free time and get plenty of opportunities to love on furry pals. If you cannot have a pet of your own, offer to walk a neighbor or friends' pets.

- **Learn about exotic pets and get yourself one** – There are plenty of animals within the animal kingdom to choose from when it comes to picking out a safe pet. From fish, birds, reptiles and even tarantulas (if you are into that sort of thing..) there are pet stores you can find them in.

- **Learn a new language** – While there is no way to turn back the time physically, there are always new ways to keep your brain young and vibrant and to keep your mind peaked. Learning a language is a great way to dust off the many cobwebs of your mind and acquire a skill. If you plan to visit a country where they do not speak your language, this can be a great initiative to learn one!

- **Be an usher at a theater or concert** – If you love the theater or listening to music but think the ticket prices are ridiculous, perhaps this would be a good little gig for you! Volunteering your ushering services can usually land you free door fees. Each theater or concert has different policies, so be sure to check in before landing yourself into a volunteer position of this kind that may have no benefits.

- **Become a museum or zoo guide** – This is another great volunteer opportunity that you can take up! Find a niche that you are passionate about or wish to learn more about and find a museum, gallery or zoo near you that may be taking volunteer applications to become a knowledgeable guide. This is very rewarding as you are learning and then teaching others what you have learned!

- **Go back to school** – When you were more youthful you may have thought about hitting the books again to attend college or finish up a degree, but never had the chance to. No matter how old, knowledge is power! There are actually many programs that offer college for free for people who are seniors.

- **Renew old friendships** – This can certainly be either an indoor or outdoor activity. If anything, aging teaches us that life is short. Retirement is a superb time if any to treasure old connections and get back in touch with those that used to mean so much to you. With the help of the World Wide Web, it is now far easier to find past pals and make plans to get together. Reach out to old buddies, attend class reunions, etc.

- **Mentor a small business** – There are small businesses of many kinds that wish they had someone overseeing them that had the knowledge to help them get ahead. You can be a great asset to booming businesses by providing your know-how and expertise! It is important that in some shape or form that retirees pass on what they know to the next generation to keep it afloat and to keep building a community of successful entrepreneurs.

Retirement Activities that Result in Income

- **Sell crafts on Etsy** – If you love to create things that peak the interests of others enough for them to purchase, perhaps spending some time setting up an online store on Etsy, Ebay or other websites would be of interest to you! Instead of letting all your creations add up and take up room in your house, sell them for other people to enjoy! It is a great way to make a few bucks for something you already love doing!

- **Drive a school bus** – While you might have to fish out some change in order to receive the correct type of commercial driver's license needed to operate a school bus, this can be a very rewarding part time gig that can take up some time almost all year round. If you love and are compassionate about children, this could be the perfect side hustle for you!

- **Get a roommate** – Yes, this idea sounds quite orthodox, but there are plenty of retirees that are widows or single and who become lonely over time during their retirement years. If you have the space in your home to do so, why not invite someone to share your living space with and earn a little cash on the side?

- **Drive a truck** – For those that wish to travel and still earn some money along the way as they take in sights from around the country, driving a truck can be rewarding!

- **Work at a local pet store** – This is another great option for seniors who are not allowed to have pets or are unable to take care of one themselves. Pet stores typically have pets to care for within them that are available for purchase. If you are capable of loving them without becoming too attached, this could be a great gig for you.

Cheap Places to Live during Retirement

If part of your retirement means starting somewhere fresh to enjoy your time of leisure and relaxation. The only challenge is finding somewhere that is a nice location that fits within the means of your budget and fixed income. This chapter is full of the cheapest places to spend your retirement!

Bakersfield, California

Why not spend your golden years basking underneath a California sun? With all the perks of Cali and affordable living, you cannot beat this town! Average rainfall is 6.75 inches and there is a whopping 272 days of sunshine each year!

- Annual amount for groceries: $3220
- Annual amount for rent: $7,000
- Annual expenditures: $42,071

St. Louis, Missouri

There are many awesome services that proudly serve senior citizens and retirees in the friendly St. Louis community. One of the best entities is the St. Louis County Age-Friendly Community Action Plan that provides volunteer drivers for those that need to get around when they can no longer drive on their own, calls to check in on senior health, home repair, legal assistance and tax preparation are also included! There are also many historical sights to see and feast your eyes on!

- Annual amount for groceries: $3210
- Annual amount for rent: $7225
- Annual expenditures: $42,049

Gainesville, Florida

Located in the middle of Florida, this town is the home of the University of Florida and Lake Alice, a natural reserve that you can spend lot of time seeking out gaters, bats and turtles, just to name a few species.

- Annual amount for groceries: $3,138
- Annual amount for rent: $7,188
- Annual expenditures: $41,996

Columbia, South Carolina

In this region of South Carolina there are many retired seniors lining up to move here. With the amazing recreation and parks departments there is a lot to offer regarding activities.

- Annual amount for groceries: $3,397
- Annual amount for rent: $7,419
- Annual expenditures: $41,885

Phoenix, Arizona

If the beautiful weather filled with warm winters, hiking and amazing golf courses is not enough to satisfy you, Arizona is also a state that does not tax Social Security income. Ensure that if deciding to move here that you are ready to a feel of a bigger city and metro areas. Also, pack lots of sunscreen. Arizona enjoys more sunshine each year than parts of Hawaii.

- Annual amount for groceries: $3,058
- Annual amount for rent: $7,523
- Annual expenditures: $41,837

Austin, Texas

Austin is one of the most rapidly expanding cities in the U.S. While it is made up of a series of suburbs, there is a nice small town feel to Austin. You will definitely need a car in working order to ensure that you get to see all parts of this growing city.

- Annual amount for groceries: $3,085
- Annual amount for rent: $9,085
- Annual expenditures: $41,739

Dallas, Texas

This city has a grand low cost for living expenses and its suburbs are sprinkled with a variety of stellar places for retirees of many ages to enjoy. Dallas has all the things big cities have, like pro sports, zoos and lots of world-class dining opportunities.

- Annual amount for groceries: $2,963
- Annual amount for rent: $8,417
- Annual expenditures: $41,708

Pensacola, Florida

At the far western end of the Florida panhandle lies Pensacola. If you want a nice taste of the beach for your time in retirement, this town is for you! Lots of sunshine and beaches to be enjoyed.

- Annual amount for groceries: $3,255
- Annual amount for rent: $7,276
- Annual expenditures: $41,541

Sioux Falls, South Dakota

Healthcare in Sioux Falls is more than affordable and all the sights to see such as aquatic centers, miles and miles of hiking and biking trails and parks are a big bonus.

- Annual amount for groceries: $3,319
- Annual amount for rent: $7,151
- Annual expenditures: $41,421

Ann Arbor, Michigan

If you're looking for somewhere with a bit more of a youthful feel to retire to, this town is the perfect place for you! It is a college town full of young populations and has many great college sports team events.

- Annual amount for groceries: $2,973
- Annual amount for rent: $8,321
- Annual expenditures: $41,276

Tulsa, Oklahoma

Tulsa is known as the city of lakes and has many beautiful gold courses to enjoy your afternoons at!

- Annual amount for groceries: $3,263
- Annual amount for rent: $7,392
- Annual expenditures: $41,055

Salem, Oregon

Salem has been in the top 100 places to live in the world thanks to its natural amenities, cultural and recreational options, as well as affordable health care. Oregon is also another state that does not tax Social Security income.

- Annual amount for groceries: $3,111
- Annual amount for rent: $7,310
- Annual expenditures: $41,046

Madison, Wisconsin

If you are planning to live solely off your Social Security of pension, you will be thrilled to hear that Wisconsin doesn't tax either of these incomes. There are five lakes, 260 parks and more than 200 miles of path and trails to tread.

- Annual amount for groceries: $3,105
- Annual amount for rent: $7,994
- Annual expenditures: $41,041

Kansas City, Missouri

There are many great transportation options to travel around this city and in 2016 came up in the list of most affordable places to live at number 19.

- Annual amount for groceries: $3,045
- Annual amount for rent: $7,366
- Annual expenditures: $40,984

Rochester, New York

If you want to retire somewhere that is not hot or cold all year round, Rochester has 4 distinctly beautiful seasons. The average temperature during the summertime is 78 degrees and in the winter it is 32 degrees.

- Annual amount for groceries: $3,067
- Annual amount for rent: $7,421
- Annual expenditures: $40, 586

Salt Lake City, Utah

This city stands 4,330 feet above sea level and is home to many ski areas. This is somewhere where your family will for sure want to visit you during the holiday season!

- Annual amount for groceries: $3,066
- Annual amount for rent: $7,619
- Annual expenditures: $40,529

30 Fun-Filled Days of Retirement Challenges & Activities

Day One

"And so the adventure begins."

It is time to pick somewhere you have always wanted to visit, whether it is just a few miles out of town, across the country or in an entirely different country! Look at your funds and see how much you have and are willing to spend on a trip. And if you have a spouse, don't forget to include them as well! After deciding where you want to do, decide what kind of activities you wish to participate in and experience while you are there to get the most out of your trip. Plan alongside your partner and make the planning portion fun!

- *Why are you traveling?* – ask yourself why you want to travel in the first place. Is it just to get a photo in front of the Grand Canyon or is there a deeper personal meaning you wish to fulfill?

- *Value your hard earned dollars* – If you put more meaning behind your travel you have a much better chance of your traveling experiences to be rewarding and memorable.

- *Who are you traveling with?* – If you are traveling with family, sit everyone down and discuss each other's interests. The best memories are made when each person in the group gets to experience what they love. If you are traveling with your spouse, talk about individual desires in order to make decisions that will suit the both of you.

- *What kind of trip do you have in mind?*
    - Adventure
    - Relaxation
    - City or country
    - Beaches
    - Mountains
    - Resorts
    - Road Trips
    - Festivals/other cultural experiences
    - Shopping/food
    - Luxury
    - On a Budget

- *How much time do you have?* – decide how much time you have to actually travel. This will help you to come to a conclusion where you want to go.

- *What is your budget?* – It's easier than ever before to come to a traveling decision based upon your budget. Consider the strength in which your earnings can travel so you can get the most bang for your buck.

- *What seasons do you prefer?* Hate the snow or major heat you reside in now? Take a break from it! Travel to somewhere that currently has the climate that you prefer, so you can really enjoy your experience.

Day Two

"What do you call a person that is happy on a Monday? Retired."

If you are at the beginning of your retirement era, there is no need to jump right back into another job. You have spent so much time in your life dedicated to work, building a foundation to live off of as you age and become older. Use some of that money up by looking into investing some of it to make a profit down the line! There are many websites that can assist you or a trip to the bank can help you decide where to put your money in order for it to grow.

- Put some of your earnings into a retirement account if you haven't already. Many people's employers have a 401(k) or 403(b) plan, which are great options that are allowed to grow tax free.

- Put money aside into a tax-advantaged retirement account of your very own, such as an IRA.

- Invest money into a regular account

- Invest in the stock market or penny stocks

Day Three

"Retirement: When you stop living at work and start work at living."

Is there a specific thing you are passionate about that you have not had the time to engulf yourself in previously while you were working? Today is the day to take the steps to get into your passion head on. Like to write and wish to write a book? Start journaling every day. Like to fish? Once a month go on a fishing expedition by yourself, with a loved one or with family.

- Write memoirs during down time

- Write letters to family and friends

- Take up a new hobby that you are passionate about or wish to learn more about.

- Spend time with family and friends you have not had time to see in ages.

Day Four

"Often when you think you're at the end of something you're at the beginning of something else." – Fred Rogers

If you have always wanted to start a business but never had the time of the funds to do so, this is your last shot to make that dream come true! No matter how big or small the business is, take a leap! Turn your hobbies and interests into something that you love to do, and it will never seem like work.

- Try out online ecommerce websites to sell homemade goods, ebooks, etc.
- Become an affiliate marketer
- Find a retail space in your city to open up a business that you have always wanted to run.

Day Five

"The best is yet to come."

It is time to hit the books a bit again and learn something new and exciting that has always interested you! Earn that second degree. Expand the mind. Knowledge is power and you are never too old to acquire new things.

- Search online websites that allow you to take virtual classes
- Check into your local colleges to see what their schedules and programs have to offer you
- Check into local classes that your city is hosting and participate

Day Six

"Keep Calm: It's my last day of work."

Dig around in your attic or storage room and dust off that old guitar or other instrument that you haven't touched in years. It is time to play a few strings and get the hang of it once again. And if you never really learned? Get yourself a tutor, sign up to attend a music class, buy yourself a how-to book.

- Check out a 'how-to' book from your local library or purchase one online

- Participate in a musical learning class where you can learn from an expert along with other participants.
- Watch YouTube videos and other tutorials to gather needed information

Day Seven

"Retirement is not the end of the road. It is the beginning of the open highway."

Learn a new art/craft! Whether it is painting, drawing, crocheting, printmaking, anything that grabs your attention or that you are interested in learning!

- Spend one night a week going to an art class where others are learning the same skills.
- Utilize websites such as Pinterest to gather ideas about crafting and read/watch 'how-to' tutorials to gain an understanding of the hobby.

Day Eight

"I don't know where I'm going from here, but I promise it won't be boring."

And if you do not want to learn how to do art yourself, why not learn how to be an art critic! While there is quite a bit of know-how that goes into being a true critic, anyone with the right creative and open mindset can do it!

- Shadow an art teacher or well known art critic to gain experience
- Actively participate in open art shows to gather new insight, personal experience and an understanding for different kinds and mediums of art.

Day Nine

"This is the beginning of anything you want."

If you are ready to catch some more Vitamin D from the warm rays of the sun, perhaps creating your own garden to tend to would be a great start! Even if you are not one that loves to be outdoors, you can make your own indoor garden as well. Just make sure you have room for one so that it gets plenty of sunshine.

- Invite friends and family to help you create a garden in your own yard or on your own patio.
- Gardens do not have to be huge! Live in an apartment of assisted living? Make you own mini garden by taking care of potted plants, zen gardens, etc.

- Get the community involved! Talk to the mayor or other important city folks about setting up a garden club for people of many ages to participate in.

Day Ten

"Doing what I want, when I want: Retirement."

Host a picnic or potluck with family, friends and neighbors!

- Have a weekly potluck or gathering with those you love with good food and good conversation.
- Host a themed evening once a week. Have people dress up and actively participate for prizes to make it more fun!
- Bring the neighborhood together by making a dedicated day of the week to gather at the park or other public place in your neighborhood. This will help you develop new friendships.

Day Eleven

"You know all those things you have always wanted to do? You should go DO them."

Decided to live away from civilization during your retirement? Perhaps it is time to gather some chickens, some cows, some horses, goats..the works for a farm! While it is hard work, having fresh eggs and cow's milk will be worth the trouble. And you can sell it too if you wish!

- This idea allows you to branch out and experience a new way of living. If you have resided in a city your entire life, the country life is one that retirees like to experience, for its slow pace. Plus, it is awesome to produce your own goods with a little bit of hard work.

Day Twelve

"Relax. Entertain. Travel. Indulge. Read. Enjoy."

Get out of the house and visit a new club, bar or restaurant and order something that you wouldn't normally get on a regular basis.

- Dust off that good for nothing phone book at search for new places to eat and experience new culture.

- Invite family and friends to tag along with you to festivals, tastings, new business openings, etc.

Day Thirteen

"Let the recess begin!"

Join a club! It can be a book club, chess club, church club, any club! As long as it gets you out and about, communicating with other people and getting you involved in something that is fun for you!

Day Fourteen

"How lucky am I to have something that makes saying goodbye so hard." – Winnie the Pooh

If you have a funny bone, perhaps it is time to sign up for open mic night! Make your community laugh with your wit and humor.

- Having trouble coming up with material that you could use for comedy night? Take the time to watch a few open mic nights and enjoy them!

Day Fifteen

"Retire from work but not from life."

Join a choir! It is time to share your voice to more than your shower walls.

- There are many church choirs, college choruses, etc that are always looking for people to join their groups. Even if you feel you are not very talented, there is nothing that you cannot learn from watching and participating from these groups.

Day Sixteen

"Retirement: Where every day is a Saturday!"

Start a blog. What are you passionate about? Find a niche and write on your blog each day! Don't worry; there are plenty of resources to help get you started. IF your spouse is interested, let them write posts too! You can also make lots of money from this idea if done right.

- There are lots of websites and resources that can easily help anyone to start their own blog. Write about your passions, expertise, anything!

Day Seventeen

"You are retired not expired!"

Lobby for a cause! Is there something that you wish you could change? Gather members of the community that feel the same and rally up! You could potentially make a change for the better!

- First, look for local causes that are searching for people to fight
- Gather people in your neighborhood and educate others about your passions
- If none in your local area, invest some money in helping other causes around the world that you are serious about.

Day Eighteen

"Whatever's good for your soul: Do that."

Become a master of star gazing! While telescopes can be on the expensive side, if you are really interested in learning more about the nights' sky, it's worth every penny!

- Take a class where you can learn more about space, the stars and the alignments of the planets
- Teach your grandkids about your findings

Day Nineteen

"You are never too old to set another goal or to dream a new dream..." – C.S. Lewis

Check out a museum or gallery. If you feel you have the expertise to enter a gallery, by all means, go ahead!

- There are plenty of museums that if not in your city, you can travel to. Make a list of places you are interested in visiting.
- Educate your grandkids about places you wish to visit and have them tag along
- Look into galleries in your area. If you are into art and actually create your own, what are you waiting for? Sign up and enter!

Day Twenty

"My goal is to create a life I don't need a vacation from."

Search for live events that are happening near you. Attend and enjoy yourself!

- The warmer months are the best seasons for outside live events. Search your local city websites or keep an eye out in flyers.

- Many events are free for senior citizens. If you have never been able to experience certain events before, now is your shot!

Day Twenty-One

"Find the joy in the journey."

Take up puppetry or ventriloquism!

- Go to shows in your area of travel to some to get a feel for this activity. You may find that it is something you have always wanted to try.

- Once you know you have a knack for it, practice!

- Then, sell yourself. Attend kids' birthday parties and other such events with this new, entertaining skill.

Day Twenty-Two

"I hope the days come easy and the moments pass slow and each road leads you where you want to go."

Get yourself involved in how to make your own home brews and share them with family and friends.

- Find an expert or take a step into a local brewery.

- There are plenty of kits online that you can get started with and develop your brewing skills.

- There are also lots of 'how-to' books and online video tutorials to help you along

Day Twenty-Three

"I'm going to make the rest of my life the best of my life."

Go experience the many tastes of wine at a local vineyard.

- There are lots of wineries all over the country. Look up many that catch your eye. Travel to them and give your taste buds an experience of a lifetime!

- Learn more about wineries through local taste testings that many local pubs, breweries and events have.

Day Twenty-Four

"Retirement = World's longest coffee break!"

Sign up to participate on a recreational senior sports team.

- There are many different kinds of sports that are created just to suit senior citizens. Many of them were discussed previously within this book.

- Invite your other friends and family to participate in homemade games at home!

Day Twenty-Five

"The legend has retired."

Has your home become way overcrowded by all the belongings you have managed to collect over the years? If there are things that your family and friends do not wish to acquire, it is time to have a good ole fashioned yard sale!

- Many retirees decide to live in a more minimalistic style so that they can easily travel and live better within their means. De-cluttering their lives is a big part of that. Involve the whole family and the entire neighborhood. Host a neighborhood wide garage sale! Or talk to your mayor to have a city-wide garage sale.

Day Twenty-Six

"Just when the caterpillar thought her life was over she began to fly."

Master the ways of meditation and yoga.

- Sign up for a yoga class. It is not just for younger people anymore! There are plenty of similar classes for older individuals to participate in.

- Learn the way of meditation through tutorials found online of actively participate in a meditation class.

- Learn the ways of visualization so that you are better able to see your future in a positive light! Remember, retirement should not be dull and boring or seen as the end.

Day Twenty-Seven

"Retirement marks the end of working for someone else and the beginning of living for yourself."

Become a foster parent. This can be a very hard but more rewarding way to spend time helping others!

- There are plenty of resources that can help you decide if you want to take on the challenge of fostering a child. If you have yet to recover from empty-nest syndrome, perhaps this is a great way to fulfill your legacy, take up some time and help out a child in need.

- This is an especially great option for retired couples. Two is better than one of course! But do not think that just your set of hands can't handle it.

Day Twenty-Eight

"After climbing the mountain you can finally enjoy the view."

Volunteer at a shelter in your community, like animal or homeless shelters. Or volunteer at local events within your community.

- Utilizing time at an animal shelter can help you to receive some much needed furry rejuvenation as well as give attention to otherwise neglected animals who need homes. Talk to your shelter to help spread the word about adoption. Encourage people in your community to go out to their local shelter and adopt a pet in need.

- Volunteer at your local homeless shelter, helping other volunteers make meals and shelter options for the homeless in your community.

- Volunteer time at places like thrift stores and other such places that do not have the money to provide paychecks to all of their employees. You will be helping out local businesses all the while using your time wisely by helping others.

Day Twenty-Nine

"For years you've worked and slaved all day. Now it's time to relax and play. So put your feet up and take a break. You're now retired for goodness sake!"

Spend more time with family and friends. Reconnect with people you have lost touch with!

- In today's world, there are many avenues in finding people who you have lost communications with. Take a few moments during your days to hunt them down. If you cannot do it yourself, hire someone that has the capabilities to find them for you.

- Once located, spend quality time catching up with them in creative ways

Day Thirty

"Retirement is a time to look back on accomplishment as you ponder over the possibilities that lie ahead."

Plan to go on a cruise in the near future to a destination of choice!

- The biggest populations of cruises are retirees, people who have otherwise had not had the money to experience one for themselves.

- The best aspect of cruises? You can travel to multiple places during the duration of your trip that you have always wanted to visit and see!

- Ensure that you pick a cruise that you and the other people who tag along with you enjoy. The more the merrier, for you get bonus discounts when you bring more than just yourself along for the ride!

After 30 Days

This is a very small list of a few ideas to help you plan out your retirement. If only there were books that gave you something to do each and every single day for the next 20-30 years or more of leisure time you have. Sadly, our society has labeled retirement as a time for the aging to get out of the work force and do their own thing. There are many that do not consider them to be human as they are just a person in the way of the fast pace of everyday life.

Retirement is seen as the time to do nothing until you leave this planet. I hope that the insights within this book have managed to bring to light the hundreds of things you still have left to do during the last part of your life! ***Age is just a number,*** do not let it define who you are or what you are capable of doing, despite society's vision of retirees. Trust me when I say there are lots of other ideas and things to conquer than what is within this book. The chapters you have now read are just a great starting point for you to brainstorm and begin to make your journey through the bright depths of your retirement.

While it may seem like the tock is ticking, retirement is meant to be the stage of life that you slow down, live your life to its fullest potential and really soak in the rewards of all your hard work you performed throughout the main chunk of your adult life. Retirement means various things to different individuals. The world has made it possible to retire even earlier than ever before, meaning there are people as young as their 40's and 50's taking on the challenges of being a retiree. Surprisingly, there are some that are even younger than this! And there are retirees that are older than the average age of 65. Like I said, age is just a number. Retirement is no longer for the elderly and should not be viewed that way!

If you have passions you have always wanted to fulfill, destinations you have always wished you could see, time that you never had with your beloved families and new grand babies, retirement is the time to do all the things you wish you had done, no matter what limitations you think will hold you back. Granted, if you are in you 90's perhaps climbing Mt. Everest is not the best way to spend time. But if your heart tells you that you must, I am certainly not here to hold you back in any way, shape or form. There are many things that our souls tell us we must complete in order to die content and full of happiness.

Whether that be traveling the globe or finally getting in contact with an old high school buddy of yours, your retirement is *yours*. That's right! No one can tell you how to spend the last but not least stage in your life, not even those government checks. You have learned that it is important to spend your time wisely. Well, the bulk of retirees today more than likely did not get to do that for the majority of their life. They step into retirement with greased, callused hands with a pocket less full of cash than they like. They go into retirement thinking everything will happen as it should without much thought. Retirement is work, in a sense, but the greatest kind! You are now your own boss, fulfilling your life's legacy with things that also bring your soul prosperity, peace and harmony.

So whether you want to live our the remainder of your life helping others, teaching others what you know well, learning a new skill, molding magic with your hands in the form of arts, crafts, etc., travel the world and document as you go or simply make your neighborhood a better place for all its residents, no retiree should have to sit at home, bored out of their gourd and wondering what the world to do with the many remaining years of life they still have left ahead of them. At least no after you have read the entirety of this book!

My dear friend, welcome to retirement! I hope that the contents of this book are able to treat you well as you step into the final but the most fun, fulfilling and fruitful stage of your life *yet*! It is all up to you to make the rest of your years count, so what are you waiting for? Good luck in everything that your retirement brings to your life!

Conclusion

Thank you for making it through to the end of *Retirement*!

I hope that the contents of this book were fun to read as you discovered all new ways to utilize the ample amount of time you are about to have! I hope that you were better able to visualize your life in a happier manner than what so many people view retirement age as. You have a right to thoroughly enjoy the years of leisure that you have worked so hard your entire life for.

I hope that the chapters within this book were informative and able to give you the tools you need to start having a bit of fun in your life. No matter how old you are, age is just a number when it comes to having fun and enjoying yourself! I hope that the newly acquired information you have soaked in will lead you to achieving everything you wish to do during your last stage of life.

The next step is to put some of the ideas, challenges and activities to the test to see which one you enjoy the most, which ones suit you and which ones provide you with the perhaps the most fulfillment you have received out of your life so far.

You have worked hard to successfully make it to retirement, now it is time that your retirement worked for you! While this stage of life is meant for you to slow down, it shouldn't mean living a life full of boredom and lack of color. It is time to do some of the things that you wish you had time for during your younger years. While the activities in this book provide you plenty of ideas to start out, the world is your oyster as you venture into this stage of life. Remember that your life is not over, in fact in ways, it is *just the beginning*. You are only bound for success as long as you continue to see life in a positive way and venture to new explorations! Good luck as you journey into your time of retirement. And furthermore, enjoy it to the fullest potential!

Finally, if you found this book useful in any way, a review on Amazon is always appreciated!

Free membership into the Mastermind Self Development Group!

For a limited time, you can join the Mastermind Self Development Group for free! You will receive videos and articles from top authorities in self development as well as a special group only offers on new books and training programs. There will also be a monthly member only draw that gives you a chance to win any book from your Kindle wish list!

If you sign up through this link http://www.mastermindselfdevelopment.com/specialreport you will also get a special free report on the Wheel of Life. This report will give you a visual look at your current life and then take you through a series of exercises that will help you plan what your perfect life looks like. The workbook does not end there; we then take you through a process to help you plan how to achieve that perfect life. The process is very powerful and has the potential to change your life forever. Join the group now and start to change your life!
http://www.mastermindselfdevelopment.com/specialreport

Printed by BoD in Norderstedt, Germany